This book belongs to:

____

24 23 22 21 1 2 3 4

Published by Tughra Books
335 Clifton Ave.
Clifton, NJ, 07011, USA
www.tughrabooks.com

ISBN: 979-8-89729-507-4

Mini Muslims Series ISBN 9781597849692

WHAT IS Islam?

Islam is our religion.

It is to submit yourself to God.

We believe in only One God, Allah.

He is our Creator.

He is the most Kind, Powerful, and Loving.

Allah sent many prophets to share His message

and show us how to live.

The last prophet

He sent was Prophet

Muhammad (pbuh).

We follow his example.

Allah also sent down many books to teach us how to worship Him.

The last book He sent was the Quran.

People who follow Islam are called Muslims.

There are over one billion of us!

We love

Islam!